Tuckers' Gold

L.L. Owens

Illustrated by Tim Jones

Rigby®

A Harcourt Achieve Imprint

www.Rigby.com
1-800-531-5015

Literacy by Design Leveled Readers: *Tuckers' Gold*

ISBN-13: 978-1-4189-3798-0
ISBN-10:   1-4189-3798-3

Printed in China
1A 2 3 4 5 6 7 8 985 13 12 11 10 09 08 07

Contents

First Crossing

April 16, 1849

The morning dawned bright and clear. The wagons of the Jackson expedition— one hundred families starting west from St. Joseph, Missouri, to seek new lives and fortunes in the gold fields of California— headed for the Missouri River, where the expedition would make its first crossing. But when they arrived at the river landing, they found that they weren't alone. Another wagon train was already waiting to cross. The wagons up ahead would go first, but they had been waiting for a week because of heavy rains. The river was too high for them to cross.

"I had no idea it would be so crowded," Penny Tucker remarked. "I guess we'll be waiting a while. After we get settled, I'll make myself useful. I'm sure there's work to be done."

"What do you want me to do, Ma?"
12-year-old Penny asked her mother. She
wanted to keep busy. It would help keep
her mind off the home she was leaving.

"We'll divide up chores for the trip,"
Ma said. "That way we'll know our
responsibilities. First, though, let's
fix dinner."

Sam, Penny's younger brother, called
his Uncle James back to the wagon from
the riverbank, where he had been looking
things over. The family sat down to a meal
of bacon, cold beans, and coffee. They
would be eating a lot of beans on their
long journey to California.

The Tuckers—Penny, 11-year-old Sam,
their mother, and their father's brother,
James, were beginning the biggest
adventure of their lives.

The family had sold the store that Penny's father had opened a few years before, and they were traveling by covered wagon to California. Penny's father had gotten sick the previous spring, and the doctors couldn't save him. That had been hard for Penny and her family, but they'd tried their best to keep the business going.

When two new stores had opened in their town, though, the Tuckers found that they could no longer stay in business. Uncle James, who had made a living as a traveling artist, painting portraits and maps for wealthy customers, returned to the family with an idea.

Gold had been discovered in California— lots of it! People were heading west by the thousands to find their fortunes. Uncle James, who had promised his brother that he would take care of his family, thought it was time for the Tuckers to head west and find their fortune, too.

Now the Tuckers, just like everyone else in the expedition, thought of themselves as '49ers, fortune-seekers who traveled west in 1849 to find gold.

After dinner the family agreed on chores for the journey. Ma would cook, milk the cows, and do the mending. Uncle James would steer the wagon, hunt, and take his turn with the other men on guard duty. Sam would feed the animals, and Penny would help cook and do the wash.

That night a restless feeling spread through the camp. People were disappointed by the delay. "Getting the gold" was on everyone's mind.

"We need to cheer this group up," said Uncle James as the Tuckers sat by the fire. In a rich, deep voice, he started singing. Soon men from neighboring tents joined him. Their performance was rewarded with hoots, hollers, and applause. Uncle James grinned, bowed, and lifted an imaginary hat from his head.

Then people started trading stories about gold. One man claimed that all Californians kept barrels of gold with flour scoops inside for easy access. Another said that people drank from gold cups and ate with gold forks.

Finally, cheered by music and tall tales, the camp settled down for the night.

After five long days, it was time to cross the Missouri River.

Everyone was bustling around, eager to get under way. People wrapped tents around poles and stashed them in the wagons, rounded up their livestock, emptied their coffeepots, and stomped out their fires. They were ready.

The time came for the Tuckers to cross the river. Uncle James guided the oxen. Penny, Sam, and Ma watched. They would cross in a small ferryboat.

They cheered when the wagon's back wheels safely reached solid ground. But as it pulled onto the trail, Penny observed, "Some people seem sad today, Ma."

"I think the trip is becoming real now to most of them," said Ma. "California is a long way off, and there's no turning back now. We're all on our way."

San Francisco

September 1849

They had reached the West at last!
After long weeks of heat, dust, coyotes,
thunderstorms, spoiled food, lost livestock,
rattlesnakes, and even a tense meeting
with Cheyenne warriors on horseback,
the Tuckers and the other members of
the Jackson expedition had arrived in San
Francisco.

"We made it!" exclaimed Sam, breaking
the silence.

"We did indeed!" said Uncle James. "I
was beginning to think this day would
never come."

Uncle James guided the wagon up to
one of the many wooden buildings on the
muddy street. "This is it, the Simpson
Boarding House. Our friend Mr. Endicott
back in Missouri wrote to Mr. Simpson.
They're friends from way back. He
arranged for us to stay here."

"I wonder what it's like inside," said Ma. She had heard tales of San Francisco's boarding houses. Many were little more than huts in which lots of men crowded each night for a hot meal and an uncomfortable night on one of the shelf "beds" that lined the walls.

"This looks nice, Ma," said Sam, "like a regular house."

Ma relaxed. "Yes, it does, Sam," she said. "Shall we knock?"

Penny rushed to the door. As she raised her hand to knock, the door swung open. A family came out carrying their belongings and waving to a man standing just inside.

Penny had never seen people like these before. She was fascinated.

The woman nodded politely. It took a moment for Penny to realize that the woman was nodding at her. Penny had been staring at the woman's dark, almond-shaped eyes, milky fair skin, and gleaming black hair pulled up and wrapped around sticks. She was Chinese, Penny decided. When the woman smiled, Penny blushed. She hadn't meant to stare.

The man inside the door called out, "Good luck! Let me know when you're open for business!" Then his gaze went to Penny and her family. "Hello, miss," he said. "Are these fine people with you?"

Uncle James held out his hand. "I'm James Tucker. Are you Mr. Simpson?"

"I am. Call me Charlie, please," he said. "I like to keep things simple."

"Thanks, Charlie," said Uncle James. "I believe Mr. Endicott in Missouri told you to expect us."

"Yes, the Tuckers from Missouri!" said Charlie. "I understand that you'll head off in search of gold, Mr. Tucker, and the rest of the family will board here. Come in!"

The family stepped into an inviting living room. The house was spacious and well furnished. It was dustier than Ma might have liked, but she felt at home for the first time in months.

Charlie said, "The house is mighty empty right now, and a bit dirty. My helpers quit a few weeks back. But I've got clean rooms for you. You're my only boarders, so I could manage that on my own."

"What happened?" asked Uncle James. "I thought every boarding house in the city would be full."

"Word got out that I'd rented a room to foreigners," Charlie replied. "That Chinese family stayed here a few weeks, and folks didn't like the idea, including the couple who worked for me. The Chinese family paid their bill and was very polite. I'll take customers like them any day."

Uncle James helped the family unload things and settle in. By early afternoon, though, he was ready to leave. Penny knew all along that he would go straight to the gold fields, but now it seemed so sudden.

"Uncle James?" she asked. "Why not start out fresh in the morning?"

"I'm riding with other men from our expedition," he replied. "We'll buy our gear this afternoon, travel this evening, and start looking for gold tomorrow morning."

As he mounted his horse, Ma wiped away a tear. "Be careful, James," she cautioned. "We need you back in one piece!"

"Write often!" said Sam. "I want to hear all about the gold fields."

"Don't forget about us," added Penny.

"No chance of that happening!" Uncle James exclaimed. "I'll visit as soon as I can. Take care of each other!" With that, he was on his way.

Penny awoke the next morning to the smell of coffee. She yawned, stretched, and wondered, "What's different about today?" She rubbed her eyes, and then it hit her: the coffee's aroma wasn't mixed with the smell of smoke, or earth, or livestock. "I'm in San Francisco, and I slept in a real bed!" she thought.

Penny remembered that the family needed to look for work. It would be a while before Uncle James could send money from the fields. She dressed and hurried downstairs. Everyone else was already in the kitchen. Ma had made herself at home and was cooking up a huge breakfast.

"Good morning, Penny," Ma said. "We're about to eat."

"Ma, this looks wonderful," sighed Penny. She sat on a bench and helped herself. After months of beans, hotcakes tasted heavenly.

"How did you sleep, Penny?" asked Charlie.

"Fine, thank you, sir," she answered.

"Good," he said. "Your brother was up before dawn. He has the fever."

"Fever?" echoed Penny, looking at Sam with concern.

"Yep," laughed Charlie. "Gold fever. It's going around."

"Well, I have the cure," said Ma. "Who would like a second helping?"

Everyone enjoyed breakfast. Charlie put down his fork and said, "You were right, Mrs. Tucker. Hotcakes are a cure for the fever. Who'd want to rush out the door and miss them?"

"Tell us about gold fever," Penny urged.

"A lot of people are catching it," Charlie chuckled. "Sometimes I dream about closing the boarding house and heading for the fields myself. Sometimes I just dream about gold, period. When I hear about someone finding gold, I'm jealous. It's like it's *my* gold they're finding."

"I'm surprised you're still here," Penny said. "Uncle James caught the fever 2,000 miles away. You're right next to the gold fields."

"Not many I know are still here," said Charlie. "Shops shut down. Newspapers stop publishing. People leave town nearly every day."

"Is the city getting smaller?" Sam asked.

"No. Even more people are coming to San Francisco. It's growing fast. That means opportunities for folks like you."

"What sorts of opportunities?" Sam asked. "We need work—right, Ma?"

"Charlie made a generous offer last night," Ma said with a huge grin. "He wants to travel, so he asked us to run the boarding house. In exchange, we can live here for free."

"Your mother wanted to know how you children felt," Charlie said. "So, I hope you'll say yes. Mr. Endicott speaks highly of you. I could sure use your help."

"It sounds terrific," Sam said. "Don't you think so, Pen?"

Penny glanced at Ma before answering. "It's wonderful. Thank you, Charlie."

Charlie said, "It's settled. Together we'll run the best boarding house in the West."

"We'd best get to work," said Ma. "We have to clean this place up!"

Penny's new life in San Francisco had truly started.

A Full House

"When do you think our first boarders will arrive?" Penny asked Charlie a few days later.

"Tomorrow, for sure," Charlie said. "We'll have plenty of business. Some people have come knocking the past few days while we were cleaning. We have room for 15 men. And Simpson's Boarding House charges a fair price."

"What's fair?" asked Sam.

"Some places charge five dollars a night! Everything in San Francisco is expensive. But I don't take advantage of people. We can charge two dollars and still make money."

"That'd be more than two hundred dollars a week!" exclaimed Sam. "You'll be rich!"

"It'll take plenty of work to earn that money," Ma said. "It'll be harder than running the store."

"But we're in business," Charlie said.

After breakfast the next day, Penny, Ma, and Sam walked to the market. Carts and animals filled the streets. Everywhere merchants traded with customers. There were shopkeepers from all over the world. So many different languages could be heard that it was almost a surprise to hear English.

After buying supplies, the trio walked over to their favorite shop. It offered all sorts of unique things. Today, Penny and Ma admired a smart Spanish hat while Sam picked out some writing paper. When they returned to the house, six dusty-looking men were waiting. "They're gold miners," Penny decided. Each wore sturdy boots, and she saw a pickax strapped to the back of one mule.

"Howdy," one of the men said. "My friends and I heard you were offering beds at two dollars a night."

Another man said, "We also heard that you have real beds."

"That's true," Sam answered proudly. "At Charlie Simpson's Boarding House we don't believe in crowding folks."

"Come on in," said Ma as she opened the door.

"We're just in from the gold fields," the first man said.

"Did you see our uncle?" Penny asked excitedly. "He's James Tucker, from Missouri. He's tall and thin and he has dark brown hair."

"I can't say I did," the man chuckled. "There are so many men, it's hard to remember who you meet."

"Supper is included with your room," Ma said. "We're having beef stew, biscuits, and apple pie for dessert. I hope you'll like it. We'll call you when supper's ready."

The exhausted miners headed upstairs. Soon, the sounds of snoring men drifted downstairs to the front room.

"Can you believe our luck?" Penny asked. "Six boarders! I hope business keeps up."

"We'll do fine," Ma said. "But we can't expect a full house right away. It'll take time for folks to hear about us."

There was a knock on the door. Penny ran to answer it. Three men stood outside.

"Beds for two dollars? Is that right?" asked one of the men, as all three walked in.

"That's right," said Penny. "Each room sleeps three."

"We'll take one!" the men almost shouted.

"That only leaves us two empty rooms," said Ma. But by the end of the afternoon, the boarding house was full, and Ma and Penny were cooking for a crowd.

Sam rang the supper bell at 7:00 P.M. Fifteen hungry men filed downstairs and ate every bit of stew, biscuits, and pie. Afterward they sat with Charlie, drinking coffee and swapping stories.

Penny and Sam listened, but Penny found herself yawning. As long as the boarders were up, the family was on duty. Then a question from one man caught her attention. "Who here has seen the great elephant?" he asked.

Several muttered, "I have!"

"Are there elephants in the gold fields?" Sam asked in a low voice.

"They must be talking about the circus," said Penny.

The man smiled at his audience and said, "I'll explain. Once, a farmer decided to go see the circus after selling his fresh vegetables at the market. On the way to town, he met the circus parade led by a big, gray elephant."

He continued, "The farmer was excited, but the elephant scared his horses! They bolted and his wagon tipped over. All his vegetables were ruined. The farmer said, 'I don't care. I have seen the mighty elephant, and he was worth it!'"

"Since then," another man added, "people say they've seen the elephant when they mean they've seen it all."

"But when someone says it out in the gold fields," said Charlie, "it means he's ready to give up!"

Several men nodded their heads. Apparently they'd had enough searching for gold. The conversation turned more serious as the men discussed their plans. Some were just taking a break, but others were leaving the fields for good.

"People seem so desperate to get here," Penny said. "But you say you're leaving!"

"Mining is a hard life," one man answered. "I wish I hadn't come. I lost my money and gave up a year of my life because I thought I could get rich."

"Some people have made fortunes," said Charlie. "You just need the right kind of technique."

"I think it's mostly luck," said the man. "I didn't have any myself. After six months of panning for gold, I have less money than when I started."

"Has the gold run out?" Penny asked. She was beginning to worry about Uncle James.

"No," Charlie said. "There's still gold to be found out there. I know it."

"That's true. I found gold most days," still another man said.

"Then why give up?" Penny pressed.

"At first," the man said, "I figured I'd strike it rich. Now, I have another plan. I want to have a shoe shop here, like I did back East. There should be plenty of business. Everybody needs shoes, and I'll get rich by providing them!"

Penny shook her head. "After coming all this way, why would you want the kind of life you had before?"

"It's not the same. We're building a new town here."

It was true, Penny realized. San Francisco had grown and changed every day since she had arrived.

"You're right about making it here as a businessman," said Charlie. "That's what I'm doing with my boarding house." Then he shook his head slowly. "Still, I'd like to try the gold fields someday. I'm going to do some traveling starting next week. The Tuckers will do a fine job running the boarding house while I'm gone."

News from the Gold Fields

December 1849

Penny shivered. It was a cool, rainy December morning. She and Sam were running errands, but she was tired of slogging along the wet, muddy roads.

"It's delivery day," said Penny. "We should pick up the mail."

At the post office, the two children eagerly examined their parcels and letters. Penny's face lit up when she recognized the handwriting on one letter.

"Here's a letter from Uncle James!" she said. "It's been weeks since we've heard from him."

"And look," said Sam. "We have one from Charlie, too."

Charlie had been gone for a month. He hadn't told them where he was going this time, but he had seemed excited.

"Let's get these letters home to Ma," said Penny.

Back at the boarding house, Ma opened Charlie's letter first. She shook her head and laughed.

"Charlie warned us that he had a case of gold fever. Listen to this."

She shared the letter, which was dated two weeks earlier.

Dear Tuckers,

I have some big news. I'm out in the gold fields! I didn't tell you where I was going because I didn't want you to talk me out of it. I have the "fever." I still want to travel the world for a time, once I've made my fortune.

I know that you will continue to run the boarding house while I'm gone. It's good to have people there I can trust.

Fondly,
Charlie

Ma's hands shook as she put down the letter.

"What is it, Ma?" asked Penny.

"I wonder what he'll do with the boarding house. If he sells it, we may be out of a job and a place to live."

"Oh," said Penny. "I hadn't thought of that."

"Well, there's no point in worrying about it yet," said Ma. "What does Uncle James have to say?"

"Maybe he struck it rich!" exclaimed Sam.

Penny began reading.

Dear Family,

How is everyone? Did you receive the gold I sent last time? It wasn't much, but it's the best I could do. I'm sorry I haven't written for a while. It took me some time to save for paper.

I'm still working with men from the Jackson expedition, but I'm moving soon. I'd like to try my luck closer to San Francisco so I can visit more often.

I work from sunrise to sunset every day. The conditions are rough. There's a lot at stake for the men who promised their families they would return wealthy.

I was robbed the other day. There's a lot of thieving out here. You learn not to talk when you make a good find. That attracts the wrong kind of attention.

I miss you all. I hope to visit soon, and to send more gold—I just need to find the right spot!

Love,
James

Penny said, "I wish Uncle James would come back."

"Why?" asked Sam. "He's busy looking for gold!"

"James feels bad about having to close the store in Missouri. He wants to succeed in California and keep his promise to your father to take care of us," Ma said.

"Well, I miss him," Penny sighed.

"Is that so?" asked a familiar voice from the doorway.

"Uncle James!" Penny and Sam cried.

Something Unexpected

"Here's another piece of pie, Uncle James," said Penny. "I saved it from supper." She put a plate on the table in front of her uncle. The dining room was empty except for the Tuckers. All the boarders had gone to their rooms for the night.

"Thanks," Uncle James said. "I shouldn't eat another bite, but it's so good."

Penny was worried. Uncle James was even thinner than he had been. He seemed tired—and sad, too.

"We got a letter from Charlie," Sam said as his sister took a seat beside him.

The fork paused on its way to James's mouth. He looked from Sam to Penny to Ma.

"We got it today, along with yours," Penny added.

"Charlie's looking for gold!" exclaimed Sam. "Isn't that great?"

"Yes," said Uncle James. Penny was confused by his lack of excitement.

Now Ma joined in. "He isn't too interested in the boarding house anymore. He wants us to run it for now, but I'm worried about what the future holds for us. I'm not angry at Charlie for wanting to find gold, though," she added.

"It seems that you're all doing a wonderful job. I wouldn't worry," James said. He hesitated, and then he looked at Penny and Sam and his eyes dropped. He forked up a piece of pie and chewed thoughtfully.

"How long are you home?" asked Ma.

"As a matter of fact," said Uncle James, "I've decided to leave the fields. I was waiting for the right time to say so, and now seems as good as any."

"I'm glad," said Ma softly.

"So am I!" said Sam. "But I still think you could've struck it rich."

James continued, "I've seen a lot of tragedy in the fields, and I'm ready to get back to a normal life. I'm not sure what I'll do, but I'll figure something out."

Penny suddenly felt cheated. "That's it?" she cried. "You're done with gold? You dragged us to this horrible place—and now we're stuck? I can't believe it!"

"Penny!" Ma said sternly. "You will not speak in that tone."

Penny already regretted her words. "I apologize, Uncle James. I had no right to say such things. And I really am glad to have you back."

James stood up and put his arms around his niece. Penny welcomed his hug, but it didn't change how she felt. After all this, it seemed that leaving home had been completely unnecessary.

"I wanted things to be different, Penny," James said. "I wanted to make it big in California. I'm sorry you don't like it here, but I think we can make a good life for ourselves."

"Charlie will know what kind of work you can do," Sam said.

Uncle James let go of Penny and sank into a chair. "Charlie is another reason I came back," he said heavily. "I have some sad news. Charlie's camp wasn't far from mine, and I heard that he was at the gold fields.

Then last week a man came with a message from Charlie. As soon as I saw the man's face, I knew he bore bad news. Sickness had swept through the camp. Many miners died—including Charlie."

Ma gasped, and Sam's grin disappeared. A tear slid down Penny's cheek.

"Charlie had one last wish," James continued.

"The boarding house?" Ma whispered.

"Yes," James said. "He left it to the family." He looked into three sad faces and added, "This family, I mean. He said that you had become his family. He wanted you to own the boarding house."

At last Ma spoke. "James," she said, "this is too much. Charlie was our friend. He helped us stay together. I don't know what to do."

Uncle James looked at Penny and said, "Maybe you won't even want to stay in San Francisco. Selling this house would give us enough money to go back East."

The four of them sat for another hour. They talked about Charlie and all his kindness. Then James told about his own experiences as a miner.

"It's hard," he said. "Most days I spent hours standing in ice-cold water up to my knees. I'd dig and dig and end up with only a fleck of gold in my pan. Then I had to do it all again. Gold is getting harder and harder to find."

"You did the right thing by coming back," said Penny. She wanted to erase the memory of her earlier outburst. "We've had boarders who've done the same thing."

"Eventually you realize that the dream isn't worth the risks," admitted James. "I think I've talked long enough. It's time you children got to bed."

Over the next few days, Uncle James learned his way around San Francisco as he looked for a job. He knew he could be useful at the boarding house, but he wanted to do more.

"Please, James," Ma said. "Take your time. You need to think things through. It's a big decision."

"You're right," James said. "I need to figure out my next move."

His favorite head-clearing activity had always been painting, so James bought a few supplies. Soon the back parlor had become an artist's studio.

Penny peeked in one evening while her uncle worked. He stopped painting when he noticed her.

Penny stepped up to look. "That's our neighborhood!" she exclaimed. "I feel like I'm standing right on the street!"

"Thanks," James said. "That's the idea."

"Are you going to sell it?" Penny asked. She looked around at several other small canvases leaning against the walls. Most of them were paintings of life around San Francisco or on the trail. "You could sell these, too."

"No. I'm just fiddling around. I don't suppose anyone would want to buy these paintings," James said.

"I'll bet people would, and I'm not saying that because you're my uncle. They are really good, Uncle James!" cried Penny.

"Uncle James seems so content," Penny thought as she walked off. "More than I have seen him since before Pa died. It would be nice if he could paint all the time, like he used to do."

Trouble on the Street!

Penny headed down to the kitchen before dawn. It was her turn to start breakfast for the boarders. Yawning, she began cracking eggs into a large bowl. Penny's mind was busy, though. She was thinking about how to keep Uncle James painting.

Ma and Sam joined her, and soon breakfast was nearly ready.

Then someone pounded at the back door. Before anyone could move to answer it, the door burst open.

"Fire!" a man shouted. "There's a big fire on Kearny Street!"

"Where?" asked Uncle James, who had just come in. "How fast is it moving?"

"It's just up the road. It's moving fast, too, and spreading in both directions. I've never seen a fire like this! It could burn the whole city!"

James grabbed his hat and said, "Sam, wake the men upstairs. We'll need all the help we can get."

Penny could hear cries of "Fire! Fire!" ringing through the air outside.

The boarders ran out to the street. There was no time to waste.

"Ma, will the fire spread here?" Sam asked.

"I hope not," Ma replied. "We should get out of the house, though. These wooden buildings go up quickly." They all grabbed coats and hurried through the back door.

Outside, orange flames shot up into the sky. The air was filled with thick, black smoke. It seemed as if the entire city was on fire. The wood-framed buildings and canvas tents burned like dried grass.

Uncle James formed a bucket brigade on Kearny Street. Penny, Sam, and Ma took their places. They passed bucket after bucket of water toward the fire. The smoke made it hard to see and even harder to breathe. Sam tied a handkerchief around his mouth and nose.

The fire continued to creep closer to the boarding house. They needed more water! They could slow the fire down, but they couldn't stop it.

Then a man gave an order to start pulling down buildings. If they couldn't stop the fire, they had to take away the wood that fueled it!

Uncle James and Sam helped the other men. Horrified, Penny and Ma watched as they used ropes to pull down the building five doors away from the boarding house, then the one four doors away. Then three, then two . . .

Penny began to cry.

Then the men stopped. The fire was out! An entire block of Kearny Street was gone —all the buildings, everything—but the city was safe. And so were its people.

The crowd cheered and hugged one another. Penny threw her arms around her mother. "Oh, Ma," she said, "I was so scared."

"So was I," said Ma. "But we're all right. And so is our house."

Sam and Uncle James approached, their faces black with smoke. Together, they went into the boarding house.

All the smoke had done damage, but things could have been much worse. Uncle James moved to the back parlor to check on his paintings.

Most were soot-covered, even some that had been stacked behind other paintings. "Here's the one you liked so much, Penny. The painting of the neighborhood," Uncle James said sadly. He was looking at a large canvas. The colors were now dulled by soot.

The sight of the damaged painting made Penny feel ill. The picture had been beautiful—and now . . .

"It's gone," she said sadly. Penny was surprised at her feelings. Today she had seen the promise of a new city—her city—almost go up in flames. She had felt her neighbors' pain at losing their homes. And she had fought hard to save her own. "I guess this place has kind of grown on me," she said.

"We'll rebuild what was lost," said Uncle James.

"I hope so," murmured Penny. And she realized how much she wanted to help make that happen.

A Job for Uncle James

The next few days were very busy. The Tuckers and others who had been spared did all they could to help the people who had lost their homes and belongings in the fire. They offered beds, clothing, food, and a helping hand. The boarding house became a temporary shelter to people whose homes had been lost to the fire. Every room was filled. Some men even slept on the parlor floor for a few nights.

There was more than enough work to keep Penny busy.

"That's it," she said, placing the last clean dish in the cupboard after dinner. She was the only one helping Ma tonight, as Sam was running an errand.

"Thank you," said Ma. "Why don't we go and talk with Uncle James and the others?"

"This neighborhood is like a big family," Penny thought. In the parlor, a bearded man was just finishing his tale of sailing around South America on his way to San Francisco. Someone said, "What about you, James? What did you do before catching the fever?"

Uncle James laughed. "I was a painter. I traveled all over Missouri. I painted just about anything people asked me to."

"Including fences?" asked one fellow with a grin.

"I didn't have to do that," laughed James.

"Uncle James is a real artist," Penny announced. "Would you like to see some of his work?"

"I sure would," said the bearded man.

"So would I," said another. Several others agreed.

Uncle James held up his hands. "It's bad enough that they have to listen to my stories, Penny. Don't bore them by making them look at my paintings. Besides, the smoke damaged most of them."

"Nice try, James," said the bearded man. "We want to see your paintings!"

Uncle James gave in. "Penny," he said, "since you started all this, you go choose something."

Penny got her favorite painting—the one of the neighborhood. James had cleaned it up as best he could. Penny held it so everyone could see.

"What do you think?" she asked. "Isn't it terrific?"

"I had no idea I knew a true artist," said the bearded man. "That scene is so real it breaks my heart to see it."

"Mine, too," said an older man. "Would you consider selling the painting to me, James? I'll give you twenty dollars for it."

"What else can you show us?" asked another man.

Before Uncle James could protest, Penny said "This way to the James Tucker Art Studio!"

Soon offers were flying. "I love this portrait of Penny and Sam," one boarder said. He pulled a small package from his pocket and unwrapped a tiny plate of metal with a faded image of a little girl. "Could you use this to do a portrait of my daughter?"

"I'll give you twenty dollars for this map of the Oregon-California Trail," said the bearded man. "I know at least a dozen people who'd pay the same for one."

James was stunned. But Penny could tell that he was happy. So was she. She felt she'd made something special happen.

The older man patted Uncle James on the back. "I know you've been looking for work. You could make a nice living as an artist."

"Don't get carried away," said Uncle James. "You are friends and neighbors. I don't know if I could sell my work to strangers."

"You did this for a living once before," said the older man. "What's different now?"

James shook his head. "I was a different man. I didn't have any roots, and I didn't have much responsibility. I don't want to go back to life on the road."

"You don't have to be a traveling artist," said Ma. "You can paint right here. You just need to look at it as a job."

"Ma's right," said Penny. "Please work here. I can't think of anything better!"

James laughed. "You can't, can you?" He looked around at all the smiling faces. He said, "Well, I am a '49er, and we '49ers are bound to keep trying!"

8

The Rush Is Over

Uncle James emerged from his studio one afternoon a few weeks later. He carried something under one arm. "Where is everybody?" he called. "I have something to show you."

"In here," Ma called from the kitchen, where she, Penny, and Sam were making supper.

"Is that a painting?" asked Penny.

"It certainly is," he replied. "I know that you've been trying to decide on a new

name for the boarding house. I thought of one, and Penny gave me the idea."

"What is it?" asked Ma.

Uncle James said, "It's a name that means a lot to us. We came to California dreaming of wealth and happiness, but we learned that true happiness has more to do with family. We found ourselves coming back to the kind of work we were meant to do and living the life we were meant to live."

Uncle James turned the board around.

"Tuckers' Gold!" exclaimed Penny.

"It's a perfect name, James," said Ma.

It was a sign. On one side he had painted an elephant, and the animal's trunk pointed to the lettering.

The family trooped outside. Penny watched as Uncle James and Sam nailed the sign up next to the door.

Penny couldn't believe that only a few months ago she had wanted to leave San Francisco. "Think of all the things I would have missed," she marveled, "fighting a terrible fire, helping to build a new city, meeting people from all over.

"We truly did find our gold," she thought. "Tuckers' gold."

Timeline of the California Gold Rush

January 24, 1848 James Marshall discovers gold at Sutter's Mill.

February 2, 1848 California becomes part of the United States after the Mexican War ends.

March 15, 1848 Newspapers report the discovery of gold at Sutter's Mill, but the news is not widely believed.

May 12, 1848 Sam Brannan officially starts "gold fever" in San Francisco when he waves a bottle of gold dust. Men rush to the fields.

December 5, 1848 U.S. President James Polk confirms the discovery of gold in California.

April 1849 Wagon trains begin departing from St. Joseph, Missouri, on a two-thousand-mile journey to California.

December 24, 1849 The first big fire destroys most of San Francisco.

December 25, 1849 Frederick D. Kohler and David C. Broderick organize San Francisco's first fire department.

December 31, 1849 San Francisco's population is estimated at 100,000. In 1847 the population was less than 1000.